I salute that All-blissful Madhava whose compassion makes the dumb eloquent and enables the lame to cross mountains!

OM NAMO BHAGAVATHE VASUDEVAYA

TEACHINGS OF

SRIMAD BHAGWAT PURANA

Deliverance

Sri Pawan Dev Thakur

RAM NIVAS KUMAR

MA (English), MJMC, MLISc., Dip-in-OA

Edition

2024

Copyright

Ram Nivas Kumar

PREFACE

Sanatana dharma is a universal religion. It is to be followed by all people of the world. It is a God centred religion. It is a way of life. Sanatana dharma teaches service to the whole humanity. It renders services to all creatures.

Unfortunately, people at large are getting far off this religion. They are confused in the matter of Sanatana dharma and lagging behind the knowledge of its teachings. Hence, it occurred to me spiritually that I should write a book containing teachings of this dharma to be obeyed and followed by all.

In the meanwhile, the Sanatana Dharma Jagran Manch, Durgapuri, Malighat, Muzaffarpur, Bihar, India organized a Srimad Bhagwat Katha conducted by Sri Pawan Dev Thakur Ji Maharaj (Vrindavan Wale). Dr. Shashikant Pathak, academician, Durgapuri, Malighat, Muzaffarpur appealed to a host of scholars to write and spread the teachings of the Bhagwat Katha. His appeal touched me high and compelled me much to go with the work in the interest of all living creatures.

While writing this book, I contacted several spiritual gurus, educationists, academicians and scholars of different fields for their academic support. I also consulted a lot of books on world religion and moral teachings. I especially consulted an eminent scholar of the Sanatana dharma Shri Bhavanath Jha, Research and Publication Section, Mahavir Mandir Trust, Patna who assisted me in writing this book. A young and dynamic personality Shri Anubhav Dwivedi, National Convenor, World Youth Empowerment Forum, New Delhi along with a big host of young people encouraged me to write this book. I pay my high gratitude to all of them.

We have taken utmost care while publishing this book. However, to err is human. Inadvertent errors, if any, may please be brought to our notice. Comments and suggestions are most welcome.

We are sure that this book will boost up the morale of the followers of this religion and guide them to lead a happy and prosperous life.

—*Ram Nivas Kumar*

MESSAGE

Shri Ram Nivas Kumar is a rising star in the sky of English literature. He is an ardent devotee of Lord Krishna as well. By the grace of God, he has written about one and half dozen educational books. Almost all his books are dedicated to the students and the youth of India. Now, he has composed of a book on the learning of Sanatana dharma which deserves full praise. His present book is meant for the people who believe in the eternal dharma which is a perennial source of knowledge people ever learn and follow.

This book is based on Srimad Bhagwat Purana and my deliverances in *katha pandals* on worldly and spiritual matters. The author seems to have taken much pain in writing this book. He has covered a number of topics on manners and good behaviour to be followed by all. He depicts a true picture of ancient Indian idealism by narrating the stories of Dhruva and Prahalada. He mentioned a number of pieces of sacred learning. Teachings of the Gita are also included. The book contains vivid knowledge on world spirituality. It is inspirational for the whole world.

I appreciate the thought and mind of the author. He is actually indulging in spreading good learning amongst people living in India and abroad. Shri Ram Nivas Kumar has performed a commendable job by presenting this book. His noble endeavours are highly appreciated.

I bless him to bloom in every sphere of life and pray the Almighty to shower upon him the best blessings.

—Pawan Dev Thakur
Spiritual Leader & Motivator, Vrindavan, India.

WORDS OF EXPRESSION

We are extremely glad to know that the litterateur Mr. Ram Nivas Kumar has written a book titled "Teachings of Srimad Bhagwat Purana: Deliverance Sri Pawan Dev Thakur." Actually, this is the work we ever dreamt of. This book is really the need of the hour and demand of time. Our new generation need it more essentially.

I went through the entire book. It covers several aspects of moral teachings that we need. It contains a brief description of various points of knowledge whether worldly or spiritual. Language of the book is comprehensive and easily acquirable for the common people. Chapters like—"Work is Worship", "Samskara", and "Aim of Human Life" give practical knowledge to us. Stories of Dhruva and Prahalada are heart touching. Teachings of the

Gita are a good addition to the book. Learning of the Sanatana dharma is a must for all.

Deliverance of Sri Pawan Dev Thakur is highly essential for our new generation. Sacred knowledge on different issues of life has been included to facilitate the people learn and live a happy and prosperous life.

The author has really done a beta job by writing this book. It is a good guide and high motivation for the people in India and abroad. One must read it.

We pray the Almighty for the continuity of his writing. We bless the author all success.

—Devki Nandan Thakur
Religious Guru & Preacher, Mathura, India.

CONTENTS

1

INTRODUCTION

His Highness Sri Pawan Dev Ji Maharaj has been a great devotee of Lord Krishna since his childhood. He is a great orator of Srimad Bhagwat Katha, Sri Rama Katha, Sri Devi Bhagwat Katha, Sri Shiv Purana Katha, etc. He is a great performer of Bhajan Sandhya.

He was born on 10 March, 1994 in a Brahmin family in Mumbai. He became an ardent devotee of Lord Krishna at the age of seven. He later on returned to Ayodhya with his all family.

Maharaj Ji received basic and initial worship method and *mantras* from Pandit Radhika Prasad Pandey in Bharatkunda (Nandi Gram), Ayodhya. He learnt Rama Katha and several stories of Lord Krishna from his Guru ardently. He studied Vedas, Puranas and Upanishads at self-instinct.

His father Pandit Ramakant Shastri was a spiritual story teller (Katha Vachak), astrologist and a reader of Bhagwat katha. His mother was inspired by Sri Thakur Ji (Pujya Sri Devakinandan Thakur Ji Maharaj). She wanted her son to be like Thakur Ji. She then turned to Vrindavan to Sri Devakinandan Thakur Ji where he received education in Hindi, Sanskrit, Grammar, Katha lessons and other spiritual learning. At the age of seven, he started delivering katha lessons to people of all ages. They became saturated with their sentiments. He bestows his all success and achievements to his mother.

Sri Pawan Dev Ji Maharaj wants to build Radha-Krishna temple and cowsheds at Vrindavan and different places. He wants the publicity of Sanatana dharma across the globe and circulation of its teachings amongst the masses of the world. He wants to re-establish this religion at new realm in the present age of materialism.

Sri Pawan Dev Ji Maharaj, from time to time, assists the poor and the needy and distribute amongst them clothes, foods, etc.

Sri Pawan Dev Ji Maharaj also runs a trust namely, Vishwa Sewa Mission Trust. This trust is founded in March, 2015. The trust also assists the poor and the needy individuals.

Sri Pawan Dev Ji Maharaj received his *Diksha* from Sri Devakinandan Thakur Ji Maharaj. It is a master and disciple connection. Two souls go together to unite for creating a beautiful world and healthy worldly society.

Knowledge can be obtained from anywhere but Guru Diksha has a scientific approach. It has *Kriya, Sadhana* and *Upasana*. It is a vital science. It is a science of bodily and mental energy. It is a science of sound and energy as well. It always gives good results when performed under perfect master. Your spiritual recognition is necessary. If you practise this *Diksha* for a certain years, then other *Dikshas* like *Kriya Diksha, Samskara Diksha, Sankalpa Diksha* and *Samadhi Diksha* happen to be. Every master or every sect has his own technique. *Guru Diksha* gives a chance to transcendent. After *Guru Diksha,* one can walk on the path of self-realization. After *Guru Diksha*, one can go into Samadhi. But it is all dependent upon the Guru, upon the kind of that particular Guru. In the *Diksha,* many material tools are used.

Diksha of any kind is a ceremony, because ceremony is related to body and mind. It affects the body and the mind. It is a type of mental healing. If you practise this *Diksha,* all your bad habits are removed. It has more hidden science. It really has wonderful effect on the body and the mind. Awakening to the touch of the master can make you to bloom; can make you to enlighten.

Sri Pawan Dev Ji Maharaj has attended hundreds of Vyas Peeths and delivered his sacred lectures on Srimad Bhagwat Purana in India and abroad. He has delivered his spiritual deliverances in more than two hundred cities in India and dozens of cities in the world. He has recently conducted a specially organized Srimad Bhagwat Katha in the large premises of Durga Mandir at Durgapuri, Malighat, Muzaffarpur, Bihar, India at the behest of an ardent pair of devotees namely Smt. Munni Rani and Shri Anil Kumar Shrivastava of the same locality which ended with universal success.

2
WORK IS WORSHIP

Thus teaches **His Reverence Sri Pawan Dev Thakur Ji Maharaj:** Action is our duty. Reward is not our concern. This is the first lesson which was imparted to Arjuna by Lord Krishna in the holy book, Gita. "As you sow, so you reap" is the teaching we find in the Ramayana. There is no doubt that we should work without any concern for the result. Work is not only counted in this world but counts for the next world also. Good people are always praised in this world. On the other hand, bad men are cursed everywhere. No doubt, they are famous for their bad work. It is an admitted fact that we are duty-bound to this world. We find some stories in respect of famous workers. These workers have principle aim to work. Work is worship for them. They may face anything to get their work done even at the cost of their life and get themselves safe. Such was the case with fighters for freedom.There is no life without work. Great personalities of the world have become famous on account of their work.

Maharaj Ji further teaches: Until we make an effort, we cannot even eat our food. Life is dull without work. It is useful only if we work ever. "Work" itself is worship. There is no personality without work. The successful industrialists have understood the value of work. They devoted themselves together with the work even in their life.

He further says: Work is the only concern with men while reward is the concern in the hands of the Almighty. Fortunes favour the brave. Brave persons are always famous and rewarded. All great men sacrificed themselves on the altar of work. Concentrated work was worship for them. Our first Home Minister Sardar Vallabh Bhai Patel was a great worshipper of work not only in the eyes of Indians but also in the eyes of the people of the world. You are all *Sanatanis*. And *Sanatanis* are great worshipers of work. They may uplift the standard of their lives in a true sense. You should worship your work for the first and anything else afterwards. Your work itself is worship in your life without which the life is useless.

3
WORK IS PARAMOUNT

Work is something that we do all through life. More important than the work we do is our attitude toit. From the moment we are born till we die, work is being done all the time, whether we like it or not, whether we want it or not.

Even sitting idle or lying in the bed is an activity, a work. Breathing, digesting, sleeping, working up, binding, keeping up our muscles atone, the slow process of formation of new cells and destruction of old ones- all these activities are work that go on with or without our consent. It is only in death that work truly ceases. Many people feel that they would like to return to the age of sixty and do nothing. But as long as we are alive, it is impossible to do nothing.

Having regards that work is unavoidable, we need to look at how we do the work.

Whether it is a child who is playing, a mother who is feeding her child, a housemaid who is sweeping the floor, or a physician who is saving other's lives- what is important in all these activities is our attitude. Are you doing your work with a happy, creative and a cheerful outlook, or are you constantly complaining about and wishing for something else to do? Because if you are miserably doing the work allotted to you, you are sure that you will remain miserable in whatever work you do.

Pujya Sri Pawan Dev Ji Maharaj teaches that since work and activity is unavoidable, why not do it with pleasures, with interest, with involvement and with joy? Human beings cannot avoid what is destined to happen. What is in our hand is how to react to the work that we can. When you are standing in the queue to pay your child's fees, or waiting at a government office to renew your license or passport, you have only two choices. Either spend the time relaxing and making friends with others standing in line, or spend the time irritated, angrily and frustrated. And when you are not bothered about the outcome of the work, when you have left all that to God, then you can say that work is really worship.

WHAT IS WORSHIP? Big devotees of Lord Sri Krishna, Shri Dhannajay Kumar Jha and Shri Krishan Kumar from Muzaffarpur, Bihar ask a question as to what is worship. In reply to which Sri Thakur Ji says, "Worship is offering something to God. Here, we are offering our work to God. We normally work only for our own benefit, for our own profit. When we are ready to give up this benefit and profit and accept anything that comes our way as blessing from God, then, our work becomes worship."

And if, you truly give up attachment to the results of your work that you do, becomes immaterial. You may be a cobbler, a driver, a scientist,or a politician. In a metaphysical sense, it does not matter what you do. For, you are doing without attachments to the fruits of your labour and you are free from bondage of cause and effect. And that is why, in the Bhagavad Gita, Lord Krishna urges Arjuna to fight his own cousins not for personal gains but as God's work, as his duty or dharma without getting attracted with the possible outcome. This Arjuna's work becomes worship as he was free from the consequences of his action.

AIM OF LIFE: We believe that fulfilment of desires brings hope. But we don't realize that it ultimately makes us suffer. As taught in the Vedanta, the simple story of a monk sheds light on how renunciation and detachment from desires lead us to bliss and eternal joy.

DUTY IS UPPERMOST: Uppermost means highest in place, position, rank, power or the like. Uppermost means the highest in power, predominant, the most powerful, first in force or strength. It means first in order of precedence. It means the first in a series or in order of time. We must do our duty as is the meaning of the word "uppermost".

DUTIES AND RESPONSIBILITIES OF STUDENTS:
One more devotee Shri Pradhuman Kumar Prabhu, under Paroo block, Muzaffarpur asks about duties and responsibilities of students. Thakur Ji elaborates in detail: It is estimated that nearly 15% of the total population of India consists of students. The students, therefore, constitute a great potential force capable of

leading a nation to great heights of progress or abyss of decadence. No wonder every nation spends crores of rupees for their education and proper development. The future of every nation depends on their students.

The primary duty of a student is to learn and acquire knowledge. The main duty consists of improving their intellect and widening their mental capabilities. Unfortunately, many students forget this goal and spend their school days uselessly enjoying and idling away their time. Only later they realize the result of their folly.

School is the platform wherein students learn the good traits of life such as, discipline, obedience, dutifulness, patriotism, etc. School provide numerous opportunities for the development of these qualities. It is the duty of every student to acquire fine qualities of life which will enable him/her to stand in good stead in the future.

Another important duty of the students is to prepare them for the career they want to pursue. It is in school life that the future career takes roots. During school life, one becomes aware of one's abilities, limitations and the different professions available. School life is the right time to make proper choice of one's career.

Students are the future guardians of society. It is their duty to fight against all evils existing in their society. Students have great strength to oppose these evils prevailing in society.

Students also have a great responsibility to help our less fortunate members of the society by way of social work. They can offer great services by teaching illiterate children of nearby villages, building houses for the poor people of the locality, undertaking cleaning drives, creating public awareness on various social issues, etc.

Student can also render valuable services to the nation at the time of calamities such as earthquake, floods, severe drought and accidents. Students ought to take leadership in organising quick rescue work. In fact, student organisations such as NCC and scout troops have rendered praiseworthy services to the nations at the time of national emergencies in the past and we are sure they will continue to do so in the years to come.

Thus, students can render valuable services to the cause of the nation. Theycan play a vital role in wiping out the various ills which throttle national progress and development and thereby set the nation on its rail. They are the true assets of nation.

4
WHAT IS SAMSKARA

Samskars are rites of passage in a human life described in ancient Sanskrit texts, as well as a concept in the karma theory of Indian philosophy. *Samskara* is a Hindi word used in Indian culture to denote thought process. In English, you can call it culture containing ethics and morals behaviour. It has different meaning depending on the country and society you belong to. It is to obey the rules and regulations imposed on the individuals by the particular and immediate society they live in. Cultural difference also makes the difference in their *samskara,* say something could be included in *samskara* for one population while other can disregard it.

Samskara is multiplication of virtues and division of personality defects. Multiplication of virtues means enhancing virtues of self, and division of personality defects means reduction of personality defects in self. *Samskara* also means making good or purifying in the process. We are supposed to remove our shortcomings. A thought and a related action, when repeated a member of times, create an impression of that thought and action on our mind. This process itself is *samskara*.

One who does an action only after contemplating on all its aspects is a human. There is a need to inculcate *samskara* for good thoughts and right actions. Every work what we do reflects our *samskara.*

According to Bharatiya (Indian) culture, each and every action should be virtues in nature. Eating when one is hungry is 'nature', and eating someone else's food is 'perversion'. Whereas enquiring whether everyone in the house has had food, and then only after offering the food to God and eating it as a sacrament is 'culture'. Throwing the skin of a banana after eating is an 'action'; throwing it in a dustbin is 'character' or 'nature', whereas throwing it on the ground is 'perversion'. Picking up the skin thrown on the ground to someone else and putting it in the dustbin is 'culture.'

TYPES OF SAMSKARA: *Samskara* is of two types, namely 'good samskara' and 'bad samskara.' Good thoughts and related actions, when done repeatedly, create an impression on the subconscious mind of an individual, and his attitudes become positive. Such actions are called 'good samskaras'. Bad thoughts and related actions, when done repeatedly, create an impression on the subconscious mind of an individual, and has attitudes become negative. Such actions are called as 'bad samskaras'.

IMPARTING GOOD SAMSKARA IN CHILDHOOD:
What does teaching of good values to children mean? It means teaching them values such as paying salutation to parent everyday by touching their feet, not finding fault with others, etc. If an eight year old child is instructed to touch the feet of elderly people daily, he will do it for a few days and then stop it. He won't do regularly even if he is taught the reasons behind it. However, if the parent themselves touch the feet of their elders every day, the children too will imitate them in a few days. Even they will touch the feet of their parents and grandparents. They will feel ashamed of the fact that their parents are

touching the feet of grandparents while they are not.

Thus, inculcating *samskaras* means teaching through our own righteous actions and not just preaching. Hence, these values should not be taught to them just by preaching them or by bringing them with chocolates and ice-cream, but by putting examples through our own actions.

SOME EXAMPLES OF GOOD SAMSKARAS: Since you want to become a good individual, try to develop good *samskara*. To make the difference between good and bad *samskaras* clear to you, given below are some examples:

Good Samskara*:* Getting up early in the morning, reciting "karagre Vasate Lakshmi" paying obeisance to mother Earth, paying obeisance to parents and elderly people, behaving with humility and live with everyone, maintaining cleanliness, living neatly, attending school every day, completing home work on time, helping mother in her housework, etc.

Bad Samskara: Getting up late in the morning, drinking tea/coffee, watching TV constantly, neglecting studies, back answering, unclear habits, keeping the drawer of books untidy, telling lies, etc.

ROLE OF GOOD SAMSKARAS IN THE PROGRESS OF NATION: In days of yore, all children would respect the elders. They would pay obeisance to them every day. They would recite Sanskrut Verses before having food. In the evening, the children would wash their hands and feet, light a lamp in front of the Deity and would recite *stotras* like Ganapati strotra, Ramaraksha strotra, etc. They would sleep early at night and would wake up early in the morning. This conduct would further generate good virtues in them. When compared to them, the present day children have proportionately bad *samskaras*. If good *samskaras* are instilled in the children at an early age, it will make their life happy and help the progress of the Nation.

IMPORTANCE OF GURU: At a social and religious level, the Guru helps continue the religion and Hindu way of life. Guru thus has a historic, reverential and an important role in the Hindu culture. So many are called guru, but very few are the real or true Guru. As is described in the scriptures, the true guru is a Sat Guru who knows his Self to be one with God. There is no trace of ego left in him, no sense of 'I' or "I am this person." His consciousness is infinite; his inner State is perennial *nirvikalpa samadhi.*

Imagine a clean window with the sunlight shining though it in all its brightness. The Guru is that window. The sun is God. God shines fully through a true Guru (Sat Guru) with all His power. Such a Sat-Guru alone can free the soul.

To such a Guru we can fully bow, we can offer our complete obedience, our life, our all. Saints and inspiring teachers are essential for us. We need them and should follow them. Thousands of hard devotees like Shri Paritosh Singh, Shri Rajesh Jha, Shri Manoj Kumar, Shri Jitendra Mishra, to name a few from Muzaffarpur, Bihar, consider **Pujya Sri Pawan Dev Ji Maharaj** a supreme blessing of their life. They are grateful for having a Sat-Guru like him capable of teaching and satisfying other's souls.

WHY WE CELEBRATE GURU PURNIMA: Guru Purnima (Poornima), the tradition, is celebrated not only in India but in Nepalese traditions, too.

The tradition is dedicated to spiritual and academic teachers who evolved or enlightened humans, who shared their wisdom with others with very little or no monetary explanation. To pay honour, tribute and gratitude to such a phenomenal personality, the day is celebrated every year on the full moon day (purnima) in the Hindu month of Ashadha (June-July). The festival has a great history due to which it gets celebrated by the devotees. An ardent devotee named Shri Sanjay Jha, Malighat, Muzaffarpur says that he goes to Vrindavan and bows his head down to his **Guru Sri Pawan Dev Ji Maharaj** on the day of Guru Purnima every year. He says that he gets high spiritual merit above all material gains. All the devotees should do so.

WHO IS A GURU: Guru is a Sanskrit term that connotes someone who is a teacher, guide or master of certain knowledge. In Sikhism, the Guru tradition has played a key role since its founding in the 15th century. Its founder is referred to as Guru Nanaka, and its Scriptures as Guru Grantha Sahib.

5
AIM OF HUMAN LIFE

What is the ultimate aim of human life? Human is just a living being. It does not have any particular aim. Aim in life is created by human itself for attending higher levels of needs. You will find dissatisfaction again and again because what you are aspiring for is material. The ultimate goal of life is not to achieve any material gain because this cycle for pain and pleasure in which we are after pleasure or to achieve something is nothing but the absence of pain and pleasure. If pain is not there, then again that sort of pleasure becomes pain for us. So in this whole process pain is the root cause which forces us to aspire for pleasure. Where there is pain, there is pleasure. You have got this human form of life to enquire about the supreme absolute truth. Other things are temporary in this world. We have to leave it one day. Lord Krishna says in the Bhagavad Gita: "After attaining Me, the great souls who are yogis on devotion, never return to this temporary worldfull of miseries because they attained the highest perfection." So we should aspire for the real pleasure that can be achieved by the submissive enquiry.

ULTIMATE AIM OF HUMAN LIFE: Shri Priyaranjan Jha, a big disciple of Thakur Ji and devotee of Lord Krishna, resident of Durgapuri, Road No.-2, BMP-6, Muzaffarpur wants to know about the ultimate aim of human life. Pujya Sri Pawan Dev Thakur teaches: First, we should understand that life is only a part of the spiritual journey of the soul in its quest for knowledge, enrichment, fulfilment and finally liberation or *"Moksha"*. In a life, a person goes through the learning process of schools or colleges before completing his education.Similarly, the soul crosses a number of line (rebirths) so as to experience various situations and emotions associated with them to complete its lessons towards enrichment. These situations are driven by their past *"karma"* which decides the physical and material comfort or discomfort as reward or punishment for our own past deeds. The fine goal or aim is to get sufficiently enriched after learning our lessons from various emotional situations/challenges till the soul finally understands the need for detachment. It then achieves perfection and fulfilment and merges with the supreme entity

(Brahma) finding its *"Moksha"*. Karma is an important tool which can either speed up or delay completion of this spiritual journey. Good karma will ensure that we are less distracted by the material world while bad karma has to be dealt with by paying the penalty it imposes which has great potential to distract the person from his/her inner quest. We find that people are largely driven by their ambition to be ahead of their possession of wealth. Ideally, one must be driven in the profession by the sense of duty and righteousness and accept the rewards which may come out of their efforts. This will allow them to simultaneously focus on the red intent of their lives while the good *"Karma"* will ensure that distractions in future lives are less for them.

Searching and finding God is the ultimate goal of life. Our body is the vehicle of soul. Keep your soul pure; body clean. When we want to achieve material things, we may get it but we won't be happy because we need some other things again and again. It will never end. After attaining a particular level, we should stop wishing for material gain. Just think about it.

Understand others. Understand human mind. Think about "Giving" a good loving word to someone in deep trouble. Give an appreciation when you see a winner. Donate money for food for the needy. Help someone who really needs a help. You will feel inner happiness. No need to tell others about such things. This is all cleaning of your heart and mind. When you get a "PEACE OF MIND", give that also to others.

According to the scriptures, the ultimate purpose of this human Birth and existence is to attain Self-Realization. Self-Realization knows your Divine identity of Supreme-Self. Spiritual practice of *Karma, Bhakt*i and *Jnana* Yogas are paths of Action for the body, path of devotion for the Mind and path of knowledge for the Intellect. Meditation helps in achieving this Self-Realization.

LIFE AND STRUGGLE: You have to have an ideal in life and follow that ideal till the death of your life. To know your own Self and your purpose in life is a struggle. Also, when you find purpose in life struggling to achieve, that is a real struggle.

First of all, you should learn that the real meaning of struggle can be understood by a person who has faced some kind of struggle in his life. Everyone thinks he is facing struggle in his life but what we won't understand is that being unhappy does not mean reason for struggle. We have to take a decision depending on our self-confidence. That is the only thing left that will bring us out from struggling life. Decision taken will be either favourable or unfavourable. But since we have confidence in our decision, we can turn that unfavourable decision into a favourable one.

A person can come out of a struggling situation only when he has faith in his will power and that power will pay him in enormous ways. That is the reason why some strugglers reach that peak which they have not even thought of.We all have that power but what we need is to identify it instead of abusing our luck.

Happiness requires struggle. It does not just sprout out on the ground like daisies and rainbow. It grows from the problems. The solution lies in the acceptance and active engagement of negative experience- not the avoidance of it, not the salvation from it.

6
IMPORTANCE OF BHAKTI

MEANING: *Bhakti* means devotional worship directed to one supreme deity, usually Lord Vishnu, especially in His incarnation as Lord Rama and Lord Krishna by Whose grace salvation may be attained by all regardless of sex, caste or class. It is followed by the majority of Hindus today. *Bhakti* means loving devotion to God leading to *Nirvana*. It also means personal devotion to a particular deity. Selfless devotion is a means of reaching Brahman. A popular religious movement centred on the personal worship of gods, especially Lord Rama and Lord Krishna.

IMPORTANCE OF BHAKTI: There are many ways of worshipping God. One is by listening to His praises being sung. One way is to perform *yajnas*. Another way is through pinnacle. Some knowledgeable persons delve deep into the religious texts. But for the ordinary man who cannot read and comprehend religious literature or even listen to discourse or meditate on God, there is an easy way of worship, and that is through visiting temples, and revealing his *bhakti* by worshipping God in idol form.

IMPORTANCE OF BHAKTI BASED ON THE GITA: Bhakti movement upheld the importance of devotion that is established in our scriptures. When you worship the Lord, you should not aspire for any fruit in return. Some people sacrifice work and money but they aspire for some fruit in return.

God is one. Shavism and Vashnavism worked together. To worship God, man should serve humanity having belief that we can find God by serving a fellow human being. All men are equal. We should have a strong sense of brotherhood with a firm belief that all humans are created equal irrespective of their birth and religion. There were hundreds and thousands of spiritual and religious leaders in India who had unilaterally contributed to bind our heterogeneous and diverse society into a common fold which made India great as "Unity in Diversity."

WAYS OF WORSHIP: When you worship the Lord, you should not aspire for fruit in return. Some people sacrifice work and money but they aspire for some fruit in return. Such a service is a waste. If you do Nishkama Karma Yoga, which is the service to the Lord, without expecting anything from the Lord, the Lord comes in human form and suffers for your sins. Then alone can you get rid of your sins. Other than this, there is no alternative.Either you have to pay or your father (the Lord in human form) has to pay the fine for your sins.He will bring the good results which you were supposed to enjoy in your next birth to the present. You do not know this secret and you think that you have flattered the Lord and get rid of your sins. What you do not know is that your present sins are thrown to next birth with increased interest. Your future life cycle will be full of miseries from birth to death. There, the Lord is clearer than you when you adopt the way of business with Him.

The word *Kama* means work done with selfishness. This is not correct path. The Veda says that by such work, Salvation is not obtained. Hence, the word *Kama* should not be mistaken as all types of work. Work done for the sake of God is not covered by this word.

Doing the ritual sacrifice, singing divine songs, meditation, reading spiritual books, participating in spiritual discussions, seeing the Lord's pictures, etc. are the various ways of God's worship. You can engage yourself in any way as per the convenience of your mind and external atmosphere. Similarly, you can worship God in any form as you like.

Whatever may be the form and whatever may be the way, your interest should be spontaneous love without having desire for some fruit. God likes such natural devotion only. The devotion due to interesting fruit is not natural and hence He dislikes it. As your love appears on your life partner and children in natural and spontaneous way without any force, such true love is liked by God. For the expression of true love, there is no specific place, specific time and specific way of expression.

As you are expressing your true love to your beloved issue in any place, at any time and in any way using spontaneous words, you shall worship God in the same way. If you do not aspire for any fruit from God, your worship will be natural and fruitful.

7

BHAKTI YOGA IN BHAGAVAD GITA
(The Yoga of Knowledge)

1. Krishna said to Arjuna: I taught this imperishable Karma-Yoga to King Visasvaan. Visasvaan taught it to Manu. Manu taught it to Ikshavaaku.

2. Then, handed down in succession.The Royal sages knew this. After a long time, the science of Karma-Yoga was lost from the earth.

3. Today, I have described the same ancient science to you. Karma-Yoga is a supreme secret indeed.

4. Arjuna said: You were born later. But Visasvaan was born in ancient time. How am I to understand that you taught this yoga in the beginning?

5. Krishna said: Both you and I have taken many births. I remember them all, O Arjuna. But you do not remember.

6. Though I am eternal, imperishable, and the Lord of all beings, yet I manifest by controlling My own material nature using my Yoga-Maya.

7. Wherever there is a decline of Dharma, and the rise of Adharma, O Arjuna, Then I manifest myself.

8. I incarnate from time to time for protecting the good, for transforming the wicked and for establishing Dharma, the World Order.

9. The one who truly understands my transcendental birth and activities is not born again after leaving this body and attains my abode, O Arjuna.

10. Freed from attachment, fear, and anger; fully absorbed in Me; taking refuge in Me; and purified by the fire of Self-Knowledge, Many have attained Me.

11. With whatever motive people worship Me, I reward them accordingly. People worship Me with different motives.

12. Those who long for success, worship the Almighty. Success in work comes quickly in this human world.

13. The four Varnas and divisions of human society based on aptitude and vocation were created by Me. Though, I am the Author of this system, one should know that I do nothing and I am eternal.

14. Work does not bind Me because I have no desire for the fruits of work. The one who understands this truth is not bound by Karma.

15. The ancient seekers of liberation performed their duties with this understanding. Therefore, you should do your duty as the ancients did.

16. Even the wise are confused about what is action and what is inaction. Therefore, I

shall clearly explain what action is.Know that one shall be liberated from the evil.

17. The true nature of action is very difficult to understand. Therefore, one should know the nature of attached action, the nature of detached action, and also the nature of forbidden action.

18. Attached action is selfish work that produces Kamic bondage. Detached action is unselfish work that leads to nirvana. And forbidden action is harmful to society. The one, who sees inaction in action and action in inaction, is a wise person. Such a person is a Yogi and has accomplished everything.

19. A person whose all work is free from selfish desires and motives and whose all karma is burnt up in the fire of Self-Knowledge is called a sage by the wise.

20. Having abandoned attachment to the fruits of work, ever content and dependent on no one, though engaged in activity, one does nothing at all.

21. Free from desires, mind and senses under control, renouncing all proprietorship, doing mere bodily action, one does not incur sin.

22. Content with whatever gain comes naturally by His will, unaffected by dualities, free from every success and failure. Though engaged in work, such a person is not bound.

23. Those who are devoid of attachment, whose mind is fixed in knowledge, who does work as a sewa to the Lord, all karma of such liberated persons dissolves away.

24. Brahman is the oblation. Brahman is the clarified butter. The oblation is poured by Brahman into the fire of Brahman. Brahman shall be realized by one who considers everything as an act of Brahman.

25. Some Yogis perform the yajna and worship to Devas alone while others offer yajna itself as offer in the fire of Brahman by performing the yagna.

26. Some offer their hearing and other senses in the fires of restraint. Others offer sound and

other objects of he senses in the fires of he senses.

27. Others offer all the functions of the senses. And the functions of *Prana* as sacrifice in the time of the Yoga of self-restrain are kindled by knowledge.

28. Others offer their wealth, their austerity and practice of yoga as sacrifice, while the ascetics with strict vows offer their study of scriptures and knowledge as sacrifice.

29. Those who are engaged in yogic practice reach the breathless state by offering inhalation into exhalation and exhalation into inhalation.

30. Others restrict their diet and offer their inhalation as sacrifice. All these are thy knower of sacrifice and are purified by sacrifice. Those who perform Yajna obtain the nectar of knowledge as a result of this sacrifice and attain eternal Brahman. O Arjuna, even this world is not for the non-sacrificer. How can the other world be?

31. Thus many types of sacrifices are described in the Vedas—know them all to be born from Karma or the action of body, mind, and senses. Knowing this, you shall attain nirvana.

32. The knowledge sacrifice is superior to any material sacrifice. O Arjuna, because all actions in the entirety culminate in knowledge.

33. Acquire this transcendental knowledge by humble reverence, by sincere in duty and by service.

34. Knowing that, O Arjuna, you shall not again get deluded like this. By this knowledge, you shall behold the entire creation in your own Self Lord, or in Brahman.

35. Even if one is the most sinful of all sinners, yet one shall cross over the ocean of sin by the raft of knowledge done.

36. Verily there is no purifier in this world like knowledge. One who becomes purified by Karma-Yoga, discover this knowledge within in the course of time.

37. The one, who has faith, and is sincere, and has mastery over the senses, gains his knowledge. Having gained this one, at once attains the supreme peace.

38. But the ignorant, who have no faith and are full of doubt, perish. There is, neither in this world nor in the world beyond, no happiness for the one who doubts.

39. Karma does not bind one who has renounced work through Karma-Yoga, whose doubt is completely destroyed by knowledge and who is Self-Realized.

40. Therefore, resort to Karma-Yoga and let the ignorance born doubt vanish by the sword of self-knowledge. And get up to fight, O Arjuna.

8

IMPORTANCE OF DEVOTION TO GOD

If you feel loyal and loving towards someone or something, that is devotion. Devotion means a commitment or dedication to some purpose. The word 'devotion' has a religious meaning, too, meaning "prayer offered to God."

In Hinduism, devotion is a love to a deity leading to salvation and nirvana. It is open to all persons independent of caste or sex. Devotion is a line of demarcation for those who pursue success in any field. Devotion is a deep yearning of the heart for God... To want Him is to have devotion to Him.

WHAT IS DHARMA: Dharma is a Hindu, Buddhist and yogic concept that refers to an idea to a law,or principle, governing the universe. For individuals, to live out their dharma is for them to act in accordance with this law. In Buddhism, it is said that action is the path to enlightenment. In Hinduism, dharma signifies behaviour that is considered to be in accord with the Order that makes life and universe possible. It includes duties, rights, laws, conduct, virtues and right way of living. In Buddhism, dharma means "cosmic law and order" that is also applied to the teachings of the Buddha. In Buddhist philosophy, dharma is also a term for phenomena. Dharma in Jainism refers to the teachings of *Tirthankara* (Jina) and the body of doctrine pertaining to the purification and moral transformation of human beings. For Sikhs, the word dharma means the path of righteous and proper religious practice. The dharma was already in use in the historical Vedic religion, and its meaning and conceptual scope has evolved over several millennia.

DEFINITION: Dharma is a concept of central importance in Indian philosophy and religion. It has multiple meanings in Hinduism, Buddhism and Jainism. It is difficult to provide a single concise definition for dharma, as the word has a long and varied history and straddles a complex set of meanings and interpretations. There is no equivalent single word synonym for dharma in western language.

The meaning of the word 'dharma' depends on the context. Its meaning has evolved an idea of Hinduism. In the early texts and ancient myths of Hinduism, 'dharma' meant cosmic laws, the rules that created the universe from chaos, as well as rituals. In later Vedas, Upanishads, Puranas and the epics, the meaning became refined, richer and more complex. Dharma refers to the principles that prevent chaos in society. It refers to behaviour and action necessary to all life in nature, society, family, as well as at the individual level. Dharma encompasses ideas such as duty, rights, character, vocation, religion, customs and all behaviours considered appropriate, correct or morally upright.

WHAT IS MOKSH: *Moksha* is also called *vimoksha, mukti* or *vimukti.* It is a term in Hinduism, Buddhism, Jainism and Sikhism which refers to various forms of emancipation, enlightenment, liberation, and release. In its stereological and eschatological senses, it refers to freedom from *sansara*, the cycle of death and rebirth. In its epistemological and psychological senses, *moksha* refers to freedom from ignorance, self-realization, self-actualization and self-knowledge.

WHAT IS SANSARA: *Sansara* is a Sanskrit word that means "wandering" or word with the connotation of cycle, circuitous change. It also refers to the concept of "rebirth and cyclicality of life, matter, existence". It is a fundamental assumption in Indian religion; in short, it is the cycle of death and rebirth. *Sansara* is sometimes referred to with terms of phrase of such as transmigration, karmic cycle, reincarnation, and cycle of aimless drifting, wondering or mundane existence.

The word *sansara* literally means wandering through villages to cities. It is in the sense of aimless and directionless wondering. The concept of *sansara* is closely associated with the belief that he person continues to be born and reborn in various realms and forms.

In Hinduism, *sansara* is a journey of the soul. The body dies asserts the Hindu tradition, but not the soul which it assumes to be the eternal reality indestructible and bliss. Everything and all existence is connected and composed of two things—the soul and the body of matter. This eternal soul called *'Atman'* never reincarnates. It does not change and cannot be changed in the Hindu belief. In contrast, the body and personality can change. Our current Karma impacts the present circumstances in this life, as well as the future forms, and reclaims of lives. Good intent and action lead to good future, bad intent and action lead to bad future in the Hindu view of life.

A virtuous life and actions consistent with dharma are believed by Hindu to contribute to better future, whether in this life or future lives. The aim of spiritual pursuits, whether itis through the path of bhakti (devotion, karma), Jnana (knowledge), or raja (meditation), is self-liberation (moksha) from *sansara.*

The Upanishads primarily focus on self-liberation from *sansara.* The Bhagavad Gita discusses various paths to liberation. The Upanishads offer a very optimistic view regarding the perfectibility of human nature. And the goal of human effort in our texts is a continuous journey to self-perfection and self-knowledge so as to end *sansara*. The aim of spiritual quest is to find the true Self within and to know one's soul. The *sansara* is viewed as the cycle of rebirth in a temporal word.

WHAT IS JNANA: In Indian philosophy and religion, jnana or gyana is knowledge. The idea of jnana centres on a cognitive event which is recognised when experienced. It is knowledge, inseparable from the total experience or reality, especially, a total of divine reality.

Jnana Yoga (Yoga of Knowledge) is one of the three main paths (margas) which are supposed to lead towards *moksha* (liberation from material miseries). The other two paths are Karma yoga and Bhakti yoga. Raja Yoga (classical yoga which includes several yogas) is also said to lead to *moksha.* It is said that each path is meant for a different temperament of personality.

Jnana Yoga is the path of yoga that a practitioner can follow to self-realization. It is the path of pursuing knowledge and truth. There must be a practical experimental knowledge and not merely a theoretical one. Jnana yoga is also sometimes described as the Yoga of intellect.

9

STORY OF KRISHNA AND SUDAMA

In times unmemorable, Krishna was a king and Sudama was a poor Brahmin. There was a deep friendship between them. The king was the King but the poor Brahmin did not have anything at all. Once Sudama's wife told him, "See, Krishna is your very close friend, dear friend. Why don't you go and ask him for some help." Sudama was a little shy. He said, "How can I ask a friend for something? I don't feel like doing this." But when there was no other way to go for subsistence, he decided to meet Krishna. There is a custom in India that when you go to meet somebody, you don't go empty handed. So what could he take? He had nothing. His clothes were torn. He was so poor!But then at home, he had some rice krispies. So, he packed it in a torn and dirty piece of cloth and proceeded to Krishna.

He entered the palace. It was gorgeous and beautifully decorated. Krishna was sitting on his throne, and there were so many servants around. The moment Krishna saw Sudama, he rushed towards, embraced him, washed his feet and offered him his own seat. He put him on the throne. And then Krishna asked Sudama, "What have you brought for me? Come on. Krishna is always playful with divine enlightenment. He would make fun all the time.So, He knew that Sudama was so shy that he was trying o hide his rice krispies. "How can I offer these rice crispies?"—asked Sudama. But then Krishna grabbed it and caught on, and then he went on stuffing it in his mouth. The joy of meeting his old friend was so much that Sudama even forgot to ask anything and forgot why he had come to meet his friend, and Krishna forgot to give him anything! They both forgot! When two souls meet in such a deep friendship, they forget everything.

Sudama thanked Krishna and let the palace. And it is said, When Sudama went back to his home, he found that his whole house was transformed and he had all the riches in his house. His wife was very happy. Somebody had come with a lot of gifts without asking and without giving.

So from any angle you see them, there is a totality. There is uniqueness in Krishna's personality. And that is to indicate that you are like   that. Your innermost Self has all that. Your innermost Self has all the qualities in it as the ray of sun has the entire colour in it. Through a prism, all the colours are manifested. But the same ray of light through a black, blue or red glass reflects only that particular colour. But through a prism, the rainbow comes out. And Krishna was such a prism, so clear, so full of joy. It's wonder to say that Krishna was! Krishna is because it is the eternal presence that is never lost.

Lord Krishna says: Though I am in the body, I am not this body. Though I am working through the mind, I am not the mind. I am not what you see me as. I am such more than what you perceive me as. I am present in your heart as 'You'. And anytime you need Me, you call Me. I'll be right there with you to take you out of your troubles and difficulties. You can always count on Me.

10
STORY OF DHRUVA

Dhruva is a devotee of Lord Vishnu mentioned in the Vishnu Purana and the Bhagavati Purana. The Vedic name of the Pole Star is Dhruva Nakshtra, named after Dhruva, the son of the king Uttanpada. At a very young age, Dhruva demonstrated a steadfast commitment to Lord Vishnu and he was blessed to take the position of the steadfast polestar.

Uttanpada was the son of the king Manu. After the death of Manu, Uttanpada became the king and he was married to two girls named Suniti and Suruchi where the former was the elder and the later was younger. Dhruva was Suniti's son and Uttama was Suruchi's one. The king was more attached and concerned about the younger wife Suruchi only for the fact that she was more beautiful than Suniti. Suniti was extremely possessive in nature and at times she even did not let the king see his first wife and Dhruva. One evening Suruchi was enjoying a chat with her husband and son Uttama was playing on his lap. At that time, Dhruva, son of Suniti also came there. And seeing Uttama playing, he (Dhruva) also wanted to get on to his father's lap. But Uttanpada ignored Dhruva knowing Suniti's nature. Suruchi, seeing Dhruva trying to climb, got very furious and pushed him aside and said that if Dhruva needs to climb his father's lap, he has to be born to her. She talked Dhruva to go to penance so that in his next life he may be born as her son. Poor Dhruva felt sad. Uttanpada did not even take steps to console or embrace him with love.

Uncontrollable Dhruva being very sensitive ran to his mother crying. He was sobbing. He told his mother about the happenings. Suniti's heart was touched by seeing tears in the eyes of her son. She took him in her arms, smoothed the locks of hair from his forehead, and kissed his tears away. She soothed him with soft, loving words and gentle whispers. Once Dhruva was kindled and consoled, she asked him not to grieve at the words of his steps mother. Suniti asked Dhruva not to be angry with his step mother for God is always there to take care of evil things and evil people. For everyone must pay the price for Karmas—good or bad. Then she told her son just to think the truth conveyed to him for everything is possible by the grace of Lord Narayana. And getting blessings of the Lord Narayana, is possible only through penance and prayer. With still tears in his eyes, Dhruva asked his mother who Narayana was and where can he see Him (Narayana). Then Suniti explained to Dhruva about the Almighty. But this happens only when we take refuge to the Lord. And to attain the Lord is not an easy thing, for one has to do austerity and penance for years and years. That is how rishis and yogis have realized the presence of the Almighty by their intensive devotion both physically and mentally.

After his mother went to sleep, Dhruva kept thinking over his mother's word and then decided to get out of the palace in search of Lord Narayana. So, he came out of the palace and moved forward towards the deep woods. Then, he walked through the forest for days and nights without food and water. He was crying out loudly. "Vasudeva! Narayana! Where are you?" At a point of time, he even started enquiring the lions, tigers, bears, and jackals of the forest about Narayana. As Dhruva went in search of the Lord and cried out His name, Narada, the real sage Narada, who was sitting under a tree, heard his cries by the vision of Lord. So Narada went in search of the boy and on locating him, he tried to test his earnestness. He advised Dhruva to go back to the palace where he belongs to, for this is not the age to start off in search of God. He also told Dhruva- it is the age to enjoy and one can meditate upon after he finishes all the duties in life. So Narada insisted Dhruva to get back home and have a great life. Dhruva folded his palms respectfully and said, "Revered Sage", my burning desire is to realize God and to attain the highest goal in life. Please show me the path.

Narada now knowing that Dhruva is a sincere seeker of Lord Narayana, made up his mind and taught him Japa to meditate with a free mind, the Sacred Dvaadshakshara Mantra—Om NAMO BHAGAVATHE VASUDEYAYA. He then asked Dhruva to always feel the presence of Lord with him and devote himself entirely to his worship. Dhruva was then directed by Narada to practise meditation and to perform *Tapa* at Madhuvanam located on the sacred banks of the river Yamuna. So as directed by Narada, Dhruva went to the Madhuvanam to perform his penance. Though, it was difficult for him to concentrate, he soon got himself into rigorous *Tapas.* He really started enjoying the meditation. After some time, he went into long spells of *Samadhi.* Slowly, he also started avoiding fruits and water. He then went to an extent of sipping water once in nine days. As months passed by and he was getting deeper into meditation, Dhruva got himself totally cut off the world and lost all consciousness. He stopped all movements of his body and stood poised only on the toe of one foot. The force of his penance was getting fierce and the three worlds began to rock. The earth ditched at the point where his toe pressed the ground. When he stopped his breathe in Samadhi, the breath of three world also stopped, all but suffocating the living creatures.

Finally, Lord Narayana was pleased at his *Tapa* and decided to fulfil Dhruva with his desire. So he mounted on his Garuda and landed on earth in front of Dhruva. When Dhruva opened his eyes, he was amazed to see Lord Narayana and His sparkles dazed the sight of Dhruva. Stuck by the resplendence of Sri Narayana, Dhruva could not speak a word for he was totally taken aback and prostrated in front of Him in full length. The Lord Who was pleased much with Dhruva, blessed him with His divine conch, saying that his wishes will be granted. Narayana also told Dhruva that he can join Him only after this period as human is over on the earth. Till then, he has to go and take over his father and rule his kingdom after which he will ascend to the celestial sphere, thereby joining other celestial beings like *apsara, devas* and *gandharvas* and take a permanent place in the name Dhruva Nakshatra. Saying this, Lord Narayana disappeared. Following the God's instruction Dhruva went to his country where he was welcomed by his people with great pomp. Suniti begged his forgiveness and mother Suniti embraced him with tears of Joy in her eyes.

Dhruva was not only a great devout of Lord Narayana but also a big intelligent on the earth and in the universe. He was blessed that so long as stars shine in the sky, His name will shine in the universe. You will be called a Dhruva Tara. Not only this, but also that all stars and planets will revolve around you. You will also guide the travellers from the sky whenever they forget their path.

11
BHAKTA PRAHALADA

Once there lived a king named Hiranyakashapya. Through many years of penance, he had acquired a boon that he would not die either during the day or night, either in his house or outside, by assault from either men or animal and by no weapon made of either metal or wood. The boon gave him a lot of power. So he lived recklessly and ruled ruthlessly. He had a son called Prahalada who was a great devotee of Sri Vishnu, the Lord. He would chant Vishnu's Name all the time and during all his activities.

Hiranyakashayapa was very angry at Prahalada's devotion to God and wanted his son to worship no one, but himself. But Prahalada continued in his devotion to Lord Vishnu and his father continued to harass him to change his ways.

Out of his anger at Prahalada's devotion, Hiranyakashyapa once had him thrown in boiling oil but Prahalada came out unscathed. So another time, Hiranyakashayapa had the boy thrown from a cliff, while yet another time into a fire. But each time God saved Prahalada from any hurt. This made the king even angrier.

One day he asked Prahalada, "You say that your God will protect you. Can you show me where He is?" Prahalada said, "God is everywhere." Prahalada was standing next to a pillar. So the king asked, "If your God is everywhere, is He in this pillar?" Prahalada replied, "Yes."

Upon hearing this, the king got very angry and broke the pillar into half.The very next moment, Lord Vishnu emerged from the pillar in the Avatara (form) of Narasimha, half human and half lion. It was neither day nor night (twilight time) when this happened. He lifted the king and took him neither to the threshold of the palace such that, they were neither inside nor outside the palace. Then he placed the king on his lap and killed him with neither metal nor wood, but His claws!

God is everywhere. If one chants God's name with devotion, He saves one in all circumstances.

12
THE POWER OF NAME

Once there were two brothers—Hari and Name. Hari had no interest in chanting God's name while Name was very fond of chanting the Lord's Name. Also, Hari had many bad habits like smoking, drinking, gambling, etc. while Name was quite religious and the exact opposite of Hari in habits and behaviour. One day, Name and his friend gathered and started urging Hari to chant the lord's Name at least once toget away from their constant urging. Hari chanted the Lord's name once.

Many years later Hari died. Sri Yama (the Lord of Death) took Hari's spirit and subtle body to the subtle world. While the decision was being made whether Hari was to go to heaven or hell, they came across a record of chanting the Lord's Name once in Hari's life time. So, Sri Yama asked Hari, "What is the importance of chanting this Name?" On that Hari replied, "Sorry, but I do not know the importance of this Name." Sri Yama then asked Hari to come with Him to Sri Vishnu to gain an understanding of this importance of the Name. But in an effort to delay the decision about his fate, afraid that he was likely going to hell, Hari said, "Till it is decided whether I am to go to a good soul and should be taken by special vehicle (palkhi) to meet this Sri Vishnu that you are referring to."

Sri Yama humoured Hari and indeed took him in a special vehicle to Sri Vishnu. Upon reaching Sri Vishnu's abode, Sri Yama asked Hari to come out of the Vehicle to meet Sri Vishnu. But Hari desperate to put off the decision about his fate, refused to do so, hopping that Sri Vishnu would not take the trouble to come to the vehicle. He added, "I do not know who this Shi Vishnu is, if He wishes let Him come to meet me, but I will not come out." Upon hearing this, Sri Vishnu Himself appeared in His full glory which encompasses the whole universe (Virat Rupe). Seeing the Lord in His full glory, it instantly transformed Hari into Self-Realized soul. He thus came to gain complete knowledge of the universe. Prostrating himself in Obeisance to the Lord, he prayed, "By Your nature of this word that I was so madly after. This entire materialistic world is nothing but a dream; please allow me to stay next to your holy fact. Please do not let me depart from your Blissful presence."

Repeating the Lord's Name only once and that too, without faith, brought a bad character like Hari to the Lord in his afterlife. How much benefit would one derive in his very life from constantly chanting the Lord's Name with faith?

13

IMPORTANCE OF WORK DONE FOR
GOOD CAUSE

Raman Maharshi was a great saint who lived in southern India. Devotees from the world around travelled to his *Ashrama* to receive his blessings.

One day, Raman Maharshi was pinning some leaves together to make dinner plates for the *Ashrama*. A young devotee, who was standing nearby and watching, asked, "Gurudev (a respectful way of addressing a Guru or spiritual teachers), is it not a waste of your precious time to do such a small task? Anyone else would have done this". The saint smiled and said, "My son, no work is a waste of time, if it serves a good purpose and if done in the right away." Making these plates is as important as any other task because these plates will be used to serve food in the Ashrama. Besides, you can always learn something useful from everything you do.

Moral: Raman Maharshi teaches us that no task is small as long as we approach it with the correct attitude and a good purpose. The main purpose of our life is to serve God. Hence, we should take every opportunity to serve God by gratefully participating in any available service. (Service unto Good), Sata-Seva can be one of cleaning, cooking, conducting a lecture or satsanga (spiritual meeting) or some other spiritual activity.

14

SALUTATIONS TO LORD KRISHNA

I salute that All-blissful Madhava whose compassion makes the dumb eloquent and enables the lame to cross mountains!

There were several Avataras (Incarnation) of the Lord in Hindu mythology. But the manifestation of the Lord Sri Krishna is a unique one. He is the most popular and the most beloved of all the Avataras and there is no Hindu who does not know His name.

Sri Krishna in whose veins flowed royal blood was born in the clan of Vrishnis, as the son of Vasudeva and Devaki. Devaki was he sister of King Kamsa who was cruelly and unrighteousness personified. While he was driving the chariot in which was seated his newly married sister with her husband, he heard a voice saying, "The eighth child of this couple, O fool, will be your slayer." At once he was on the point of killing his sister, but desisted from doing so, after Vasudeva, who was famous for his truthfulness, assured him that he would hand over all his children to Kamsa as soon as they were born.

Just before the birth of Sri Krishna, Vasudeva and Devaki were imprisoned and were heavily shackled. The Lord who is the Deliverer and Saviour of the people was born in a prison house in Mathura. The child was none but Vishnu, the Supreme Lord, born to relieve the earth of sin and unrighteousness and to show light and guidance to many a yearning soul. The guards fell asleep, Vasudeva was unshackled, and the doors were opened through His divine Maya, and the child was safely carried to Gokula on the other side of the Jamuna to the house of Nanda and was exchanged with his new-born daughter.

The tyrant Kamsa, as soon as he came to learn of the birth of Devaki's child, rushed to the prison house to kill his would-be slayer with his own hand, but to his utter astonishment, he saw the child to be a girl; yet remembering the prophecy, he caught hold of the babe and was going to kill her when she miraculously slipped from his hands and went up into the sky saying, "He who will slay you, is growing at Gokula." This made Kamsa furious and he ordered all the babies in Mathura and in its neighbourhood to be killed. But He Who was born to destroy sin and re-establish Dharma (religion) remained unscathed and subsequently baffled all Karma's attempts to put an end to His life. Ultimately, Kamsa who was evil and sin personified, was killed by Krishna and Kamsa's father Ugrasena was installed on the throne.

Krishna's childhood was full of miracles. For ordinary people they were so serious, but to the Lord it was all play. One day, Krishna in a playful mood ate some mud. The foster-mother, Yasoda, made Him open His mouth to remove the mud but to her great astonishment, she saw the whole universe inside. As she was marvelling at this wondrous sight, Krishna laughed and resumed His natural form. Krishna moved to Vrindavan a few miles from Mathura where His playmates were the cowherd boys and the girls, known as Gopis, chief among whom was Sri Radha. Radha forgot herself in her love for Krishna." To the Hindus, Radha's ardent desire typifies the passionate love of the human soul for the ineffable Divine Spirit."

After some years, Krishna felt the call of a new mission and came to Dwaraka, a seaside city in Gujarat. He entrusted the government of the newly-formed kingdom to His kinsmen, the Vrishnis. Though Himself a famous warrior, a wise statesman and an intelligent diplomat, He never occupied the throne. He conquered many kingdoms, but gave them over to other. Though he was often seen in the midst of intense activity, He was always calm and unruffled. Though He was always at work He was ever absolutely unattached.

Just before the memorable battle of Kurukshetra, Arjuna, seeing his elder and kith and kin ready to fight to death, became very dejected and being under delusion started lamenting. To remove that unmanliness and delusion of Arjuna, Bhagavan Sri Krishna taught Arjuna in the battle-field the immortal Gita, the Song Celestial, the perennial source of peace and bliss. The Gita which was later compiled by the great sage Vyasa consists of seven hundred Verses in eighteen chapters.

After installing Yudhisthira on the throne, Sri Krishna went back to Dwaraka, where after a time a civil war broke out among the members of the Vrishni clan. They fell upon one another and looked on as a detached witness seeing in all the fulfilment of destiny. Realizing that the time of His own departure was at hand, He restrained His mind and senses in Yoga and lay down on the bare earth under a tree, when a hunter seeing His rosy feet, from a distant, mistook them for a crouching deer and aimed an arrow which pierced the feet of the Lord. Coming nearer, the hunter realized his grievous mistake and was sorely grief-stricken, but the Lord blessed him with a smile and soon after gave up His body.

Thus the greatest of the Avataras, after fulfilling His great divine mission of eradicating sin and re-establishing religion, left His mortal soil. Though thousands of years have elapsed, the memory of Lord Krishna is ever green in the hearts of millions of devotees. May He dispel all darkness and shower His benign blessings upon all!

15

SWAMI VIVEKANANDA ON LORD KRISHNA

Lord Krishna is worshipped in various forms, the favourite ideal of men as well as of women, the deal of children as well as of grown up men... He was the most wonderful Sannyasin and the most wonderful householder in one. He had the most wonderful amount of Rajas, power, and was at the same time living in the midst of the most wonderful renunciation. Krishna can never be understood until you have read the Gita, for He was the embodiment of His own teaching.

The glory of Sri Krishna is that He has been the best preacher of our eternal religion and Vedanta that ever lived in India. In the Gita, we hear the distant sound of the conflict of sects, and Lord Krishna comes in the middle to harmonise them all; He, the great teacher of harmony, Lord Sri Krishna. He says, "In Me, they are all strung like pearls upon a thread."

16

JNANA YOGA
(The Path of Knowledge)

BLESSED are the pure in heart, for unto them is given the knowledge of God.

As the rising sun dispels the darkness of the night, so the knowledge of the Atman drives away all delusion.

The yoga of knowledge is for those who desire nothing, for they, knowing every desire to be fraught with evil, have renounced work.

Blessed is human birth. Even the dwellers in heaven desire this birth. For true knowledge and pure love may be attained only by a human being.

Seek not for life on earth or in heaven. Thirst for life is delusion. Know that life is transitory. Wake up from this dream of ignorance. Strive to attain knowledge and freedom before death shall claim to you.

The sacrifice through knowledge is superior to sacrifice performed with materials. O scorcher of foes, all actions in their entirety culminate in knowledge.

Acquire that knowledge through prostration, inquiry and service. The wise who are knower of the Truth will instruct you in wisdom.

Acquiring the (knowledge), O son of Pandu, you will no more be thus deluded; by which you will see all creatures in yourself and them in Me.

Even if you be the worst sinner amongst all sinners, you will cross all sin by the boat of knowledge alone.

As a fire well kindled, reduces fuel to ashes, so, O Arjuna, does the fire of knowledge reduce all Karma to ashes.

Verily, there exists no purifier on earth, equal to knowledge. A man who becomes perfect in yoga finds it within himself in course of time.

He who is full of faith and zeal and has subdued his senses attains knowledge. Having attained knowledge, he soon attains the Supreme Peace.

But the man who is ignorant and without faith and always has doubt goes to ruin. Not in this world, nor in the world beyond, no happiness is there for the doubting soul.

The omnipresent Lord does not accept the sin or virtue of anybody. Knowledge is enveloped by ignorance. Because of this, beings get deluded.

But those whose ignorance has been destroyed by the knowledge of the Self—their knowledge like the sun manifests that highest Being.

Fixing their minds on Him, at one with Him, abiding in Him, realizing Him alone as the Supreme Goal, they reach a state, from which there is no return, their sins having been destroyed by knowledge.

I shall tell you again the Supreme Knowledge— the best of all knowledge, knowing which all the sages have attained supreme felicity.

With this knowledge they, having attained to My nature, are not reborn even at the time of creation nor are they distressed at the time of dissolution.

Just to bless them, I residing in their intellect, destroy the darkness born of ignorance by the resplendent light of knowledge.

Humility, unostentatiousness, aimlessness, forbearance, uprightness, service to the Guru, purity, steadiness and self-control- all this is called knowledge.

Dispassion for sense-objects, absence of egoism, seeing misery and evil in birth, death, old age and disease—all this is the virtues of a man of knowledge.

Non-attachment and non-identification with son, wife, home, etc, always being even-minded whether good or evil befalls— all this is called knowledge.

Unswerving devotion to Me through the yoga of non-separation, resorting to solitude and aversion for company, always being devoted to spiritual knowledge, perception of the aim of the knowledge of Truth—all this is declared to be knowledge and all that is contrary to this is ignorance.

Learn from Me in brief, O son of Kunti, how one who has reached such perfection realizes Brahman, which is the supreme consummation of knowledge.

17

SELF (ATMAN)

But know that by which all this is pervaded, to be imperishable. No one can bring about the destruction of his immutable principle.

He who looks on the Self as the slayer, and he who looks upon the Self as slain—neither of these apprehends aright. The Self slays not, not is slain.

I (Self) is never born, nor does it ever die; nor, having once been, does it again cease to be. Unborn, eternal, permanent, and primeval, It is not slain whereas the body is slain.

Just as a person casts off worn-out clothes and puts on others that are new, the embodied Self casts off worn-out bodies and enters into others that are new.

This Self cannot be cut, nor burnt, nor wetted, nor dried. Changeless, all pervading, stable, immovable, the Self is eternal. This Self is said to be unmanifested, unthinkable, and unchangeable. Therefore, knowing this to be such, you ought not to mourn.

This, the embodied Self in everyone's body is eternally indestructible. O descendant of Bharata (Arjuna); therefore, you ought not to grieve for any creature.

The Supreme Purusha in this body is called the Onlooker, the Permitter, the Nourisher, the Protector, the great Lord and also the Supreme Self.

Some see the Self in the self by the Self through meditation, others by the path of knowledge, some others by yoga and still others by the path of action.

The Supreme Self, being without beginning and devoid of attributes, is immutable. Though residing in the body, O son of Kunti, It neither acts nor is It attached.

Just as the all pervading Akasa (ether) because of its subtlety, is not contaminated, so is the Self located everywhere in the body not contaminated.

Just as the one sun illumines the whole world, even so, O descendant of Bharata, does the embodied Self illumine all bodies.

Two birds which look alike and are friends have casually come and built their nest in a tree. One of these eats the fruit of that tree, while the other though not eating any fruit, is stronger.

That which does not partake of the fruits is wise and knows itself as well as the other; but not so the one that eats the fruits; that which is tied to ignorance is always bound, while that which is full of knowledge is eternally free.

Wakefulness, dream, and profound sleep are attributes of the intellect, being due to the Gunas. The Self is distinct from them, since it is conclusively proved to be their witness.

Last of all, meditate on the oneness of the Self with God, the one blissful existence, the One I Am.

18

SIGNS OF A STHITHPRAJNA
(A Man of Steady Wisdom)

Question: What is the description, O Kesava (Krishna), of the man of steady wisdom, absorbed in Samadhi? How does the man of steady wisdom talk, how does he sit and how does he walk?

Answer: When a man, O Partha, gives up completely all the desires of the mind, and himself delights in his Self alone, then he is said to be 'a man of steady wisdom.'

He whose mind is not perturbed by adversity, who is free from desires for pleasures, who is devoid of attachment, fear and anger—such a sage is indeed said to be of steady wisdom.

He, who is unattached everywhere, who neither welcomes nor hates, when he obtains good or evil, has his wisdom firmly fixed. When he completely withdraws the senses from his objects, as a tortoise draws in its limbs, then his wisdom is steady.

The sense-objects fall off from a man practising abstinence but not the taste for them. But even this taste of the man of steady wisdom ceases when he sees the Supreme.

The turbulent senses, O son of Kunti, forcibly lead astray the mind of even a wise man striving for perfection. Therefore, restraining the senses, the self-controlled yogi should sit meditating on Me. Verily, his wisdom is steady, and whose senses are under control.

When a person thinks deeply of sense-objects, he feels attachments for them. Attachment gives rise to desire and desire breeds anger.

From anger comes delusion which results in loss of memory. The loss of memory causes destruction of discrimination and from the ruin of discrimination the man perishes.

The man of self-control, on the other hand, moving among sense-objects with his senses under restraint, and free from attachment and aversion, attains serenity of mind. The yogi whose Self is satisfied through knowledge and realization, who is steady and has the senses under control, and to whom a cloud of earth, a stone and gold are of equal value, is said o be steadfast.

When serenity is attained, there comes an end to all sorrows. Verily the wisdom of the man of serene mind soon becomes steady. He, whose senses are well-controlled from their objects, has steady wisdom.

That person who lives completely fee from all desires, without longing, devoid of the idea of ownership and egoism, attains to peace.

Even as the embodied self attains in this body childhood, youth and old age, so does it attain another body. The wise man does not get deluded thereat.

The sense-contacts result in heat and cold, pleasure and pain. They are subject to coming and going and are therefore transient.

That wise person whom these do not afflict, who is equanimous in pleasure and pain, is fit for immortality.

He whose mind is not attached to anything, who has subdued his heart, and who is free from all longing—he, by renunciation, attains that supreme state of freedom from action.

Forsaking egotism, power, annoyance, desire, anger and superfluous things, free from the notion of 'mine' and tranquil, he is fit for becoming Brahman.

Endowed with a pure understanding, restraining the self with firmness, turning away from sense objects such as sound and abandoning love and hatred, he is fit for becoming Brahman.

Dwelling in solitude, eating but little, controlling the speech, body and mind, ever engaged in meditation and concentration and cultivating freedom from passion, he is fit for becoming Brahman.

This is the Brahmic State, O son of Pritha. Attaining it, one is no longer deluded. Being established therein even in the hour of death, one attains final liberation in Brahman.

19

BHAKTI YOGA
(The Path of Devotion)

If a meditative man constantly worships Me through the path of devotion, all the desires of his heart are destroyed, for I reside in his heart.

Hence, the practice of knowledge or dispassion is scarcely of any use to the yogi who is devoted to Me and has his mind centred in Me.

Whatever is acquired through works, austerities, knowledge, dispassion, yoga or charity, or through any other means of well-being, My devotee easily attains to it all through devotion to Me.

The man who has no desires, and cares for nothing, attains devotion to Me.

Merits and defects arising from the performance of acts, do not affect those saints who are exclusively devoted to Me.

Always praising Me, striving with austere vows and bowing down to Me with devotion, always steadfast, they worship Me.

These persons, who think of nothing else and worship Me through meditation—the accession to and the maintenance of the welfare of such ever-devout persons, I look after.

Even these devotees who, endowed with faith, worship other gods, worship Me alone, O son of Kunti, though in an unauthorised way.

By devotion he knows Me truly, how much and what I am. Then, having known Me truly, he forthwith enters into Me.

Many are the means described for the attainment of the highest good such as love, performance of duty, self-control, truthfulness, sacrifices, gifts, austerity, chastity, vows, observance of moral precepts, etc.

As fire kindled into a blaze burns the faggots to ashes, so O Uddhava, devotion to Me completely consumes all evil.

I, the Self, dear to the devotees, am attainable by love and devotion. Devotion to Me purifies even the lowliest of the low.

Let not your mind run after the things of this world, for they are empty as dreams. Give your mind to Me, devote yourself to Me, meditate on Me.

O Uddhava, neither yoga, nor knowledge, nor piety, nor study, nor austerity, nor renunciation captivates Me so much as a heightened devotion to Me.

I, the dear Self of the pious, am attainable by devotion alone which is the outcome of faith. The devotion to Me purges even outcastes of their congenital impurity.

A devotee of Mine whose speech is broken by sobs, whose heart melts and who, without any idea of shame, sometimes weeps profusely, or laughs, or sings aloud, or dances, purifies the whole universe.

As gold smelted by fire gives up its doss and gets back its real state. So the mind by means of a systematic devotion to Me winnows off its desire for work and attains to Me.

The mind of a man, who thinks of sense-objects, is adhered to them, but the mind of one who remembers Me is merged in Me alone.

Therefore, giving up dwelling on unreal things, which are no better than dreams or fancies, concentrate on Me, the mind clarified by devotion.

Arjuna said: Those devotees who, ever steadfast, worship you after this fashion, and those other who worship the Imperishable and Manifest, which of these have greater knowledge of Yoga?

The Lord said: Those who worship Me fixing their mind on Me, ever devoted, and endowed with supreme faith—them I regard as the best of yogins.

Those who renouncing all actions in Me, and being attracted to Me, worship Me with unswerving devotion, through meditation— these people, who have fixed their mind on Me, I quickly redeem from this ocean of trans-migratory existence beset with death.

Non-envious, friendly and compassionate towards all beings, free from ideas of passion and ego-consciousness, sympathetic in pain and pleasure, forgiving, always contented, contemplative, self-controlled, of firm conviction, with his mind and intellect dedicated to Me—such a devotee of Mine is dear to Me.

He, by whom the world is not afflicted and whom the world cannot afflict; he, who is free from joy and anger, fear and anxiety—is dear to Me.

He, who is free from dependence; who is pure and prompt, unconcerned and untroubled, and who has renounced all undertakings—dear to Me is the man who is thus devoted to Me.

He, who rejoices not and hates not, who grieves not and desires not, who has renounced both good and evil and is full of devotion—is dear to Me.

He, who is alike to foe and friend, unaltered in honour and dishonour, who is the same in cold and heat, in pleasure and pain, and who is free from attachment—that man is dear to Me. He who is unchanged by praise or blame, who is silent, content with whatever he has, homeless, firm of mind, and full of devotion that man is dear to Me.

Extremely dear to Me are they who regard Me as the Supreme Goal, and endowed with faith and devotion, follow this nectar—like religion.

20

KARMA YOGA
(The Path of Action)

Endowed with wisdom, giving up the fruits resulting from actions, attaining self-realisation and freed from the bondage of birth, verily, they go to that abode which is free from evil.

Established in yoga, O Dhananjya (Arjuna), perform action, giving up attachment, and unconcerned as to the success or failure.

Far inferior is work prompted by desire to work done through wisdom, O Dhananjaya. Take refuge in wisdom; those who are impelled by results of actions, are miserable.

Yoga is the skill in work, so take to yoga.The work alone you have the right, but never claim its results. Let not the result of actions be your motive, nor be attached to inaction.

Question: If you hold, O Janardana (Krishna) that knowledge is superior to action, why then, do

Thou engage me in this terrible action? Kindly tell me definitely that one thing by which I shall reach the Highest Goal.

Answer: Even of your, O sinless one, two-fold devotion was taught by Me to the world; devotion to knowledge for the contemplative and devotion to work for the active.

Not by mere abstaining from action does a man reach the state of actionlessness, nor by mere renunciation does he arrive at perfection.

The person who restrains his organs of action, but continues to dwell in his mind on the objects of the senses, deludes himself and is called a hypocrite.

But he, O Arjuna, who controlling the organs by the mind, performs Karma Yoga with the organs of action, being unattached—he excels. Perform the prescribed duties, for action is superior to inaction; moreover, if you are inactive, even the maintenance of your body will be impossible.

The world becomes bound by action unless it is done for the sake of sacrifice. Therefore, O son of

Kunti, give up attachment, and do your work for the sake of the Lord.

Know that action originates from Brahman (the Vedas) and Brahman from the Imperishable.

But that person who delights only in the Self, is satisfied with the Self, is contented in the Self alone verily has no duties to perform.

I have no duty to perform, O Partha, nor is there anything in the three worlds unattained; neither there is anything to be attained; still I am engaged in action.

Because, whatever a great man does others also copy; whatever he sets up as a standard that the world follows.

If I cease doing work these worlds would be ruined and I would be causing an admixture of castes and destroying these beings.

Therefore, always perform action which has to be done unattached; verily man attains the highest by performing action unattached.

By action alone King Janaka and others realized perfection. Even with a view to guiding men, you should perform action.

The wise man should not unsettle the faith of the ignorant who are attached to work. He should make them devoted to all work, performing action himself intently.

Actions are done in all cases by the Gunas of Prakriti. But he whose mind is deluded with egoism thinks "I am the doer."

Better is one's own duty imperfectly performed, than the duty of another well-performed. Better is death in the doing of one's own dharma (duty); the dharma of another is fraught with fear.

Work becomes consecrated and purifying when it is done as service unto Me.

He, who performs actions dedicating them to the Lord and giving up attachment, is not touched by sin, as a lotus leaf by water.

Renunciation and the performance of selfless action both lead to the Highest Good, but of the two, the performance of selfless action is superior to the renunciation of action.

It is the children and not the wise that speak of the path of knowledge and the path of action as different. Practising thoroughly even one, a person attains to the fruit of both.

The same state as reached by men of knowledge is also reached by men of selfless action. He, who sees that the way of knowledge and the way of action are one—he truly sees.

He whose actions are free from the hankering for desires and whose actions have been burnt by the fire of knowledge—him the wise call a sage.

He, who is devoid of attachment, who is free, whose mind is established in knowledge, and who does work as sacrifice for the Lord—his entire action melts away.

Verily no one becomes a yogi without renouncing desire for the fruit of action.

21
THE THREE GUNAS

The gunas—Sattva, Rajas and Tamas—which are born of Prakriti (Nature) bind fast in the body the immortal embodied Soul, O mighty Arjuna.

Of these, Sattva, on account of its stainlessness is luminous and free from evil; it binds, O sinless Arjuna, the embodied Self by creating attachment to happiness and attachment to knowledge.

Know Rajas to be the nature of passion, the source of desire and attachment; O son of Kunti, it binds fast the embodied Self by attachment to action.

But know further that Tapas is born of ignorance, and that it deludes all embodied beings. It binds fast, O descendant of Bharata, by inadvertence, indolence and sleep.

Sattva binds one to happiness, Rajas binds one to work, while Tamas, by covering knowledge, binds one to inadvertence.

Sattva manifests itself overpowering Rajas and Tamas; Rajas manifests itself over powering Sattva and Tamas; and likewise Tamas manifests itself overpowering Sattva and Rajas.

When through all the sense-openings in this body, the light of knowledge radiates, then indeed one should know that Sattva predominates.

Greed, activity, undertaking of works, restlessness, desire—these prevail, O best of the Bharatas, when Rajas predominates.

Darkness, inactivity, inadvertence and also delusion—these prevail when Tamas predominates.

The result of virtuous actions is said to be Sattvika and pure, the result of Rajas is pain, while ignorance is the result of Tamas.

From Sattva results knowledge, from Rajas results only greed and from Tamas results nothing but inadvertence, delusion and ignorance.

Having transcended these three Gunas, which are the cause of this body, the embodied self gains deliverance from birth, death, old age and pain and becomes immortal.

Arjuna said: What are the marks, O Lord, of that manwho has risen above the three Gunas? What is his conduct? And how does he rise above the Gunas?

The Blessed Lord said: He who is the same in honour and dishonour, the same to friend and foe and who has renounced all undertakings—such a man is said to have risen above the Gunas.

And he who worships Me with the Yoga of undeviating love, rises above the Gunas and becomes fit to be one with Brahman.

For, I am the embodiment of Brahman, the immortal and the immutable and of the eternal religion and absolute bliss.

Therefore, let wise men having obtained this body which is conducive to knowledge and realisation winnow out their attachment to the Gunas and worship Me. The wise meditative man should worship Me, without attachment to anything else, ever alert, and master of his senses. He should conquer Rajas and Tamas by the culture of Sattva.

With his intellect pacified, he should conquer Sattva with the help of desirelessness. By this means a man is freed from the Gunas, gets rid of his subtle body and attains to Me.

The forest is called the Sattvika dwelling; the village is Rajasic; a gambling-den is Tamasic; and My abode is beyond the Gunas.

A cheerful heart, subdued passions, a calm body, a mind unattached—know these to be the effects of Sattva. It is the gateway to the realization of My being.

A restless heart, unsubdued passions, a body frenzied with desire for action, and a mind unquiet—know these to be the effect of Rajas. A listless stultified heart, a mind ignorant and dull, a body dejected and miserable—know these to be the effects of Tamas.

When Sattva predominates, there is great illumination, when Rajas predominates, there is intense activity; and when Tamas predominates, there is unrelieved darkness.

A man freed from ego, freed from the bonds of the three Gunas, freed thus from the limitations of the mind, finds fullness of life in Me, the Brahman, the all—pervading existence.

22
THE TRIPLE DIVISIONS

Food: The food also which is liked by all is threefold, as also yajna (sacrifice), austerity and alms-giving. Do thou hear this, their distinction?

The foods that augment life, energy, strength, health, happiness and joy; and which are savoury, oleaginous, nourishing and agreeable, are liked by the Sattvikas.

The foods that are excessively bitter, sour, saltish hot, pungent, dry and burning are liked by the people endowed with Rajas, and are productive of pain and disease.

And the foods that are ill-cooked, tasteless, putrid, stale, and unclean and left over, are favoured by people endowed with Tamas.

Sacrifice: That sacrifice is Sattvika which is performed by men desiring no fruit, as enjoined by the scriptures, with their mind fixed on it, and for its own sake.

But know that sacrifice to be Rajasika, O best of the Bharatas, which is performed aiming at its fruit, as also for ostentation.

The sacrifice which is contrary to ordinance in which no food is distributed, no hymns are chanted, and no gifts made, and which is devoid of faith is said to be the nature of Tamas.

Austerity: Worship of the gods, the Brahmans (twice born), the preceptor (Guru) and the wise, purity, straightforwardness, continence and non-injury, are said to be austerity of the body.

Words that do not give offence and that are truthful, pleasant, and beneficial, and also the regular recitation of the Vedas—these are said to be the austerity of speech.

Serenity of mind, gentleness, silence, self-control and purity of heart—these constitute the austerity of the mind.

This three-fold austerity practised with great faith by men who desire no fruit and are steadfast, is said to be Sattavika.

The austerity which is practised to gain respect, honour and adoration, and which is with ostentation, and which is transitory and unstable, is said to be Rajasika.

The austerity which is practised out of foolish notion, with self-tortures or for the purpose of ruining another is called Tamasika.

Charity: That gift which is made to one who can make no return and with the feeling that it is one's duty to give and which is given at the right place and time and to a worthy person, is known to be Sattvika.

That gift, however which is given with a view to receiving in return, or looking for its fruit, or grudgingly, is said to be Rajasika.

The gift that is given at the wrong place and time and to unworthy person without regard and disdainfully, is said to be Tamasika.

Offering oblations in sacrifices, practising austerities or making gifts or anything else done without faith are called Asat (non-existent) O Partha; they fructify neither here nor hereafter.

Acts of sacrifice, gift and austerity must not be given up, but should be performed. For verily, sacrifice, gift and austerity purify the wise.

Happiness: The happiness which one relishes through practice, in which one comes to the end of all pain, and which is like poison at first but like nectar at the end is declared to be Sattvika, born of the serenity of the understanding that concerns itself with the Self.

The happiness that arises from a contact between the objects and the senses, which is like nectar in the beginning, but like poison at the end, is said to be Rajasika.

That happiness which is self-delusive both at the beginning and at the end, and which arises from sleep, lassitude and inadvertence, is said to be Tamasika.

Faith in the Self is Sattvika, faith in work is Rajasa and faith in dishonesty is Tamasa. But faith in service unto Me is beyond the Gunas.

'Om Tat Sat'—this has been declared to be the triple designation of Brahman. By that were made of old, the Brahmanas, the Vedas and the Yajnas (Sacrifices).

23

MISCELLANEOUS SACRED KNOWLEDGE

Blessed is the human birth. Even the dwellers in heaven desire this birth. For true wisdom and pure love may be attained only by human beings.

Seek no for life on earth or in heaven. Thirst for life is delusion. Knowing life to be transitory, wake up from this dream of ignorance and strive to attain knowledge and freedom before death shall claim thee.

The purpose of this mortal life is to reach the shore of immortality by conquering both life and death.

Salvation is not attained by removing the external things like kingdom, etc., but by giving up things which satisfy the flesh.

The human body is like a boat, the first and foremost use of which is to carry us across the ocean of life and death to the shore of immortality.

The Guru is the skilful helmsman; divine grace is the favourable wind. If with such means as these, man does not strive to cross the ocean of life and death, he is indeed spiritually dead.

When he realizes Me, the Self of all, the knots of his heart are loosened, all doubts cease and he is free from the bondage of Karma.

Desirelessness is said to be the highest good. Blessed, therefore, is he who has no desire.

One must be pure in heart to enter into the life of spirit. To enter purity of heart, one must observe cleanliness, practise austerities, be compassionate towards all beings, and perform the appropriate duties of life.

Verily the universe has come out of Me, and I dwell in the hearts of all beings.

Truth has many aspects. Infinite truth has infinite expressions. Though the sages speak in diverse ways, they express the one and the same truth.

If thou dost desire the highest good, thou must have poise. Maintain your equanimity even if placed in dire extremities.

Let not your peace be disturbed even if you are ridiculed or ill—spoken of by others.

Never return hatred for hatred, nor injury for injury. Desiring your highest good, you must strive to free thyself from evil and ignorance.

Let not thy mind run after the things of this world, for they are empty as dreams. Give thy mind to Me, devote thy mind to Me, devote thyself to Me, Meditate on Me.

Lean to love solitude and, ever alert, think of Me without ceasing.

Whenever, O descendant of Bharata, righteousness declines and unrighteousness prevails, I manifest Myself.

For the protection of the righteous and the destruction of the wicked, and for the establishment of religion, I come into being from age to age.

He, who knows truly My divine birth and work, is no more born after death; he attains Me, O Arjuna.

In whatever way men worship Me, in the same way do I fulfil their desire; it is My path, O son of Pritha, those men tread in all ways.

The four-fold caste was created by Me, by the differentiation of Guna and Karma. Though, I am the Author thereof, know Me to be 'the non-doer, and changeless.

The duties of Brahmins, Kshatriyas, Vaishyas and Shudras have been assigned according to the Gunas born of their own nature.

Devoted to his own duty, man attains the highest perfection.

Whatever glorious or beautiful or mighty being exists anywhere, know that it has sprung from but a spark of My splendour.

And he who at the time of death meditating on Me alone goes forth, leaning the body, attains My being; there is no doubt about this.

For whatever object a man thinks of at the final moment when he leaves his body—that alone does he attain, O son of Kunti, being ever absorbed in the thought thereof.

Therefore, at all times, constantly remember Me and fight. With mind and intellect absorbed in Me, thou shall doubtless come o Me.

One, perchance in thousands of men, strives for perfection; and one perchance among the blessed ones striving thus, knows Me in reality.

Yield not to unmanliness, O son of Pritha! Cast off this mean faint-heatedness and arise, O scorcher of thy enemies.

Triple is this gate of hell, destructive of the Self-lust, anger and greed; therefore, one should forsake these three.

Fixing thy mind on Me, thou shalt, by My grace, overcome all obstacles; but if from self-conceit thou will not hear Me thou shall perish.

The Lord (Iswara), O Arjuna, dwells in the hearts of all beings, causing all beings by His Maya to revolve, as if mounted on a machine.

Take refuge in Him with all thy heart, O Bharata; by His grace, shalt thou attain supreme peace and the eternal abode.

24
PRAYER TO LORD KRISHNA
(BY SUKA)

O Thou Lord Supreme, I bow down to Thee;
For Thy sole pleasure and play didst Thou bring
forth this universe.

Thou are the highest in the highest! Who can sing
Thine infinite glory?
Thou art the innermost Ruler of every heart;
Thou paths are mysterious; Thy ways are blessed.

Thou dost wipe away all the tears of Thy
devotees;
Thou dost destroy the wickedness of the wicked,
What sweetness is in Thy name,
What joy is in Thy remembrance!

Salutations to Thee again and again, O Lord of
hosts!
Thu art the Lord Supreme,
Thou art indeed the Vedas.
Thou art the Truth.
Thou art the goal of all discipline.

Thy lovers meditate on Thy blissful form, and
become lost in the joy thereof.
Shower Thy grace upon me, O Lord, and in Thy
mercy look upon me!

(BY NARADA)

Where the mind and the senses seek in vain to
reach Thee,
There art Thou expressed in Thy divine glory;
Thou are nameless and formless;
Life and consciousness art Thou,
The cause of all causes,
Do Thou protect us and guide us.

Like the all-pervading ether—
Thou art everywhere and within all,
Yet we know Thee not. We bow down to Thee.

Supreme bliss is Thy form.
Because of the borrowed light of Thy
consciousness—
Even as an iron gives out heat when it is near the
fire,
One realizes Thee by going beyond the senses,
the mind and the intellect.

May our hearts be drawn to Thee!